APERTURE MASTERS OF PHOTOGRAPHY

APERTURE MASTERS OF PHOTOGRAPHY

BERENICE ABBOTT

KÖNEMANN

This 1997 edition is a coproduction of Könemann Verlags GmbH, Bonner Str. 126, D-50968 Cologne and Aperture Foundation, Inc.

German translation: Elsbeth Kearful
French translation: Astride Waliszek
Typesetting: Birgit Beyer
Coordination: Sylvia Hecken
Cover design: Peter Feierabend
Production manager: Detlev Schaper
Printing and binding: Sing Cheong Printing Co. Ltd.
Printed in Hong Kong, China

ISBN 3-89508-612-6
10 9 8 7 6 5 4 3 2

Berenice Abbott was born on July 17, 1898 in Springfield, Ohio, the youngest of four children. Her parents divorced soon after her birth and she spent her early childhood separated from her older brothers and sister; she rarely saw her father. By the time she entered Ohio State University in Columbus at the age of nineteen with the idea of becoming a journalist, Berenice Abbott considered herself on her own.

Dissatisfied with her course of studies and perhaps impatient to get on with larger (if not yet definable) pursuits in her life, Abbott in 1918 accepted the invitation of a former classmate, Sue Jenkins, to visit New York. There she encountered the flourishing bohemian life of Greenwich Village where Jenkins and her husband-to-be, director Jimmy Light, were active in productions of the famed Provincetown Playhouse. Abbott did not return to college (except for one disappointing week at Columbia University, when she gave her journalism ambition one last try). For three years she supported herself at temporary jobs

Berenice Abbott wurde am 17. Juli 1898 in Springfield, Ohio, geboren. Schon bald nach ihrer Geburt ließen ihre Eltern sich scheiden; ihre ersten Lebensjahre verbrachte sie getrennt von ihren drei älteren Geschwistern. Ihren Vater sah sie nur selten. Als sie mit neunzehn Jahren an der Ohio State University in Columbus ein Studium der Journalistik begann, fühlte sie sich bereits für sich selbst verantwortlich.

Da sie mit ihrem Studium nicht zufrieden war und vielleicht höhere Ziele anstrebte, nahm sie 1918 die Einladung einer früheren Mitschülerin, Sue Jenkins, nach New York an. Dort lernte sie das lebhafte, unkonventionelle Treiben der Künstler von Greenwich Village kennen, wo Sue Jenkins und ihr zukünftiger Ehemann, der Regisseur Jimmy Light, an Inszenierungen des berühmten Provincetown Playhouse mitwirkten. Abbott ging – abgesehen von einer Woche, in der sie an der Columbia University noch einen letzten Versuch mit der Journalistik machte – nicht wieder an die Universität zurück. Drei Jahre lang verdiente sie sich ihren

Berenice Abbott est née le 17 juillet 1898, à Springfield dans l'Ohio. Elle est la cadette de quatre enfants. Ses parents divorcent peu après sa naissance ; elle passe sa tendre enfance séparée de ses frères et sœurs aînés et elle voit quasiment jamais son père. Quand, à 19 ans, elle entre à l'Université d'État de l'Ohio, à Columbus, pour devenir journaliste, elle s'estime indépendante, et seule.

Insatisfaite de ses cours et sans doute impatiente d'horizons plus vastes (sinon définis), elle accepte en 1918 l'invitation d'une ancienne camarade de classe, Sue Jenkins, à découvrir New York. Elle trouve là la vie de bohème de Greenwich Village où Jenkins, son futur mari, metteur en scène, s'occupent activement des productions du fameux Provincetown Playhouse. Abbott ne retournera à l'Université de Columbus que pour une semaine, décevante, qui sonnera le glas de ses études de journalisme. Pendant trois ans, elle vit de petits boulots de serveuse ou modèle ; elle apparaît parfois dans des productions du théâtre. Durant cette période, elle essaie de faire de la sculpture

such as waitress and model, and appeared occasionally in productions of the theater. During this time she took up sculpture, outfitting a small studio apartment for the medium. She met Marcel Duchamp when he commissioned her to cast a chess set, and his friend Man Ray, both renowned Dadaists, among other artists and writers such as Djuna Barnes, Malcolm Cowley, and Sadikichi Hartmann who were to further her introduction to the sophisticated world of avant-garde art and ideas.

After the Great War, as World War I was called, Paris enjoyed a creative efflorescence that summoned writers, painters and other artists from the continent and America. Berenice Abbott set sail for France in early 1921, intent on partaking in what was to prove one of the most exciting, creative arenas of the century. Arriving in France with virtually no money nor prospects, and speaking little French, she again supported herself with odd jobs while studying sculpture. Discouraged by her lack of success, she left Paris for Berlin in 1923, only to find that her expectations as a sculptor remained unmet.

Lebensunterhalt mit Aushilfstätigkeiten, zum Beispiel als Kellnerin oder Model, und trat auch gelegentlich als Schauspielerin auf. Während dieser Zeit begann sie mit Bildhauerei und richtete sich ein kleines Atelier ein. Sie lernte Marcel Duchamp kennen, als er bei ihr ein Schachspiel in Auftrag gab, ebenso seinen Freund Man Ray – beide berühmte Dadaisten – sowie andere Künstler und Schriftsteller wie Djuna Barnes, Malcolm Cowley und Sadikichi Hartmann. Ihnen allen verdankte sie ihre Einführung in die anspruchsvolle und hochkultivierte Welt der avantgardistischen Kunst.

Nach dem Ersten Weltkrieg erlebte Paris eine kulturelle Blüte, die Schriftsteller, Maler und andere Künstler aus Europa und Amerika magisch anzog. Berenice Abbott reiste Anfang 1921 nach Paris ab. Sie brannte darauf, auf dieser – wie sich herausstellen sollte – aufregendsten und kreativsten Bühne des Jahrhunderts mitzuwirken. Bei ihrer Ankunft hatte sie praktisch kein Geld und keine Perspektive; außerdem sprach sie kaum Französisch. Wieder hielt sie sich mit Gelegenheitsarbeiten über Wasser, während sie Bildhauerei studierte. Entmutigt von ihrer Erfolglosigkeit, verließ sie 1923 Paris und ging nach Berlin, wo ihre Erwartungen als Bildhauerin aber wieder enttäuscht wurden.

dans un petit atelier parfait pour ses matériaux. Elle rencontre Marcel Duchamp, qui lui demande de figurer sur un jeu d'échecs, et son ami Man Ray, tous deux dadaîstes connus. D'autres artistes et écrivains, comme Djuna Barnes, Malcolm Cowley et Sadikichi Hartmann l'introduisent dans le monde sophistiqué de l'art et de l'avant-garde.

Après la Grande Guerre, comme on appelait la Première Guerre mondiale, Paris avait un éclat et une effervescence créatrice qui attira nombre d'artistes, de peintres et d'écrivains de toute l'Europe et d'Amérique. Berenice Abbott embarqua pour la France au début de 1921, décidée à participer à ce qui fut reconnu plus tard comme les arènes les plus créatives et les plus délirantes du siècle. Elle arrive en France sans presque rien, sans argent et sans projets, et ne parle qu'à peine le français : elle recommence à vivre de petits boulots, les plus bizarres, et étudie la sculpture. Découragée par son manque de succès, elle quitte Paris pour Berlin en 1923, pour finalement se rendre compte que ses espoirs de devenir un bon sculpteur sont vains.

Upon returning to Paris she resumed her acquaintance with the circle of French artists and expatriate Americans who were her first friends there. In 1925, the year Abbott took up her new art, photography was beginning to enjoy an ascendency within a creative community devoted to modernism. Man Ray was supporting himself with a very fashionable and prosperous portrait studio for which he needed a new studio and darkroom assistant. Abbott challenged him to take her on when he declared that he wished to hire someone who knew nothing about photography. She took to the work instinctively, acquiring an adept technical skill and developing her eye and judgment. In a natural and evolutionary way, Abbott began to take her own portrait photographs in Man Ray's studio. Abbott soon equaled and then rivaled her mentor, setting up an independent studio with the aid of friends, including art patroness Peggy Guggenheim, in 1926. Two years later, with André Kertész and Man Ray, among others, Abbott exhibited in the first *Salon des indépendants de photographie* to considerable critical acclaim.

Sie kehrte nach Paris zurück und schloß sich wieder dem Kreis von Künstlern und dort lebenden Amerikanern an, mit denen sie bei ihrem ersten Pariser Aufenthalt Kontakt gehabt hatte. 1925, als Abbott sich ihrem neuen künstlerischen Medium zuwandte, errang die Fotografie gerade eine Vorreiterstellung unter den Avantgardisten. Man Ray war damals ein gesuchter Porträtfotograf und brauchte für sein gutgehendes Atelier und für Laborarbeiten einen neuen Assistenten. Er suchte jemanden, der nichts von Fotografie verstand – daraufhin forderte Abbott ihn auf, es doch mit ihr zu versuchen. Die Arbeit lag ihr sofort, sie eignete sich ausgezeichnete technische Fertigkeiten an und entwickelte ein gutes Auge und sicheres Urteil. Allmählich wurde es selbstverständlich, daß Abbott selbst Porträtaufnahmen in Man Rays Atelier machte. Schon bald war Abbott ihrem Mentor ebenbürtig und machte ihm sogar den Rang streitig. 1926 richtete sie sich mit Hilfe von Freunden, darunter auch der Kunstmäzenin Peggy Guggenheim, ein eigenes Atelier ein. Zwei Jahre später stellte Berenice Abbott zusammen mit André Kertész, Man Ray und anderen im ersten *Salon des indépendants de photographie* aus und erntete beachtlichen Beifall bei der Kritik.

Elle revient à Paris et reprend contact avec le cercle d'artistes français et américains expatriés qui furent ses premiers amis dans la ville. En 1925, Abbott débute dans son nouvel art ; la photographie commence à être reconnue dans cette communauté créative vouée au modernisme. Man Ray vivait de ce que lui rapportait son studio de portraits, très prospère et très à la mode : un studio supplémentaire et un assistant de chambre noire devenaient indispensables. Abbott se propose immédiatement, malgré avoir entendu dire qu'il cherchait une personne pour qui la photographie serait terra incognita. Elle se met au travail, acquiert instinctivement des techniques d'adepte et développe son œil et son jugement. D'une façon naturelle et dans la droite ligne de son évolution, Abbott commence elle-même à faire des portraits dans le studio de Man Ray. Elle devint bientôt l'égale, puis la rivale, de son Pygmalion. En 1926, elle monte son propre studio, avec l'aide de quelques amis dont la protectrice des arts Peggy Guggenheim. Deux ans plus tard, avec André Kertész, Man Ray et d'autres, elle expose au premier *Salon des indépendants de photographie* et rafle les applaudissements des critiques.

The portraits she made during the 1920's comprise a catalog of the artistic and intellectual life of that time. Their straightforward artistry masks their great subtlety; Abbott permitted each personality she photographed to project outward to the viewer. Even in the studio, where a photographic artist has the most opportunity for manipulatory control, Abbott preferred realism to guide her style.

While pursuing her own work, Abbott embarked on a decades-long crusade to promote the work of the now celebrated Parisian photographer Eugène Atget, whose passion inspired her and whose work she acquired and then diligently organized after his death in 1927. Atget had begun photographing the streets, architectural details, and gardens of Paris and environs around 1899 after a career at sea and on the stage. He made thousands of carefully annotated images from which he produced prints for sale to artists, archives and museums. Like other Surrealists, Man Ray admired Atget's photographs and shared the few he had collected with Abbott while she was still his assistant. This glimpse of Atget's vision touched her deeply: though discouraged by Man Ray from doing so, Abbott later

Ihre Porträtaufnahmen aus den zwanziger Jahren stellen einen Katalog des künstlerischen und geistigen Lebens jener Jahre dar. Hinter der Schnörkellosigkeit dieser Fotografien verbirgt sich große Subtilität. Abbott gestattete es jedem, den sie fotografierte, sich selbst zur Geltung zu bringen. Sogar im Atelier verzichtete sie auf jede Art der Manipulation und ließ ihren Stil lieber vom Realismus bestimmen.

Während Abbott ihrer eigenen Arbeit nachging, begann sie eine jahrzehntelange Kampagne, um das Werk des inzwischen gefeierten Pariser Fotografen Eugène Atget bekannt zu machen. Von seiner Leidenschaft ließ sie sich anstecken; sie erwarb seine Arbeiten und betreute sein Werk nach seinem Tode im Jahre 1927 mit großer Sorgfalt. Atget hatte um 1899 damit begonnen, Straßen, architektonische Details und Gärten in Paris und Umgebung zu fotografieren. Er machte Tausende von Aufnahmen, die er sorgfältig mit Anmerkungen versah und deren Abzüge er an Künstler, Archive und Museen verkaufte. Wie andere Surrealisten bewunderte auch Man Ray Atgets Fotografien und zeigte die wenigen, die er gesammelt hatte, seiner Assistentin Abbott. Dieser flüchtige Einblick in Atgets Werk berührte sie zutiefst. Obwohl

Ses portraits des années 1920 sont un véritable catalogue de la vie artistique et intellectuelle de l'époque. Leur coté artistique sans fioritures masque leur grande subtilité : Abbott permettait à chaque personnalité qu'elle photographiait de se projeter vers celui qui regarderait le portrait. Même dans le studio, où un photographe a la plus grande latitude de manipulation possible, Abbott préférait laisser le réalisme agir. Cette façon de travailler devint son style.

Tandis qu'elle poursuivait sa propre œuvre, Abbott mena une croisade qui dura des décennies pour sortir de l'anonymat le photographe parisien Eugène Atget, aujourd'hui célèbre, dont la passion l'inspirait et dont elle acquit et organisa tout le travail à sa mort en 1927. Atget avait commencé par photographier la rue, les détails architecturaux, les jardins de Paris et de banlieue vers 1899, après une carrière sur la mer et sur les planches. Il a fait des milliers de photographies soigneusement annotées, dont il vendait des tirages à des artistes, à des musées ou pour archives. Comme les autres surréalistes, Man Ray admirait les photos d'Atget et il avait donné quelques-unes de celles qu'il avait achetées à Abbott, au temps où elle était son assistante. Le regard d'Atget la touchait profondément ; même si

8

Jean Cocteau, Paris, 1927

began to visit Atget at home, profoundly responsive to his singular dedication to expressing the poetry of everyday reality. Just days before he died, Abbott made the only extant portraits of the master photographer [page 17]. In 1930, Abbott arranged for a volume of his photographs to be published in France and in America, and in 1964 published her own *The World of Atget,* in which she acknowledges Atget's influence on her as she extols his realism. Four years later, the entire Atget archive was purchased by the Museum of Modern Art in New York. Atget's example – his exhaustive inventory of old Paris, his uncompromising solitude, and his unwavering commitment to photography – was a source of motivation and even courage for Abbott throughout her struggle as a photographer of independent vision.

In 1929, Abbott returned to New York for a visit. Excited by the tempo of the rapidly transforming city that she had once called home, she settled her affairs in Paris and brought her portrait studio across the Atlantic. Just as it was Atget's ambition, at its most elementary, to document and preserve the vanishing Paris he loved, so Abbott was moved to record her city's transitory visage.

Man Ray ihr davon abriet, besuchte Abbott später Atget in seinem Haus. Nur wenige Tage vor seinem Tod machte sie die einzigen heute noch vorhandenen Porträtaufnahmen von dem Meister der Fotografie [S. 17]. 1930 sorgte sie dafür, daß in Frankreich und Amerika ein Band mit Fotografien von Atget veröffentlicht wurde; 1964 publizierte sie ihr eigenes Buch, *The World of Atget,* in dem sie seinen Realismus rühmt und den Einfluß auf ihre eigenen Arbeiten eingesteht. Vier Jahre später erwarb das Museum of Modern Art in New York Atgets gesamtes Archiv. Atgets Beispiel – seine gründliche Bestandsaufnahme des alten Paris, sein kompromißloses Einzelgängertum und unerschütterliches Engagement für die Fotografie – war für Abbott ein Ansporn in ihrem Kampf als Fotografin mit ganz eigener Sichtweise.

1929 fuhr Abbott zu Besuch nach New York zurück. Fasziniert von dem Tempo, mit dem ihre einstige Heimatstadt sich verändert hatte, beendete sie ihre Geschäfte in Paris und verlagerte ihr Atelier auf die andere Seite des Atlantiks. So wie Atget den Ehrgeiz gehabt hatte, das allmählich verschwindende Paris, das er so liebte, zu dokumentieren, so fühlte sich auch Abbott dazu bewogen, das vergängliche Antlitz ihrer Stadt festzuhalten.

Man Ray l'en découragea, elle alla voir Atget chez lui, consciente de sa fascination pour la poésie quotidienne. Quelques jours avant sa mort, elle fit les seuls portraits existants de ce maître de la photographie [p. 17]. Elle fit publier en 1930, en France et aux États-Unis, un premier volume des photos d'Atget, puis en 1964, elle publia son propre *The World of Atget,* où elle reconnaît l'influence du photographe sur son travail et son réalisme. Quatre ans plus tard, l'œuvre entière d'Atget fut acquise par le Museum of Modern Art de New York. L'exemple d'Atget - son inventaire exhaustif du vieux Paris, sa solitude sans compromission et son dévouement sans faille à la photographie - fut une source de motivation et même de courage dans la lutte de Berenice Abbott pour affirmer son propre point de vue photographique.

En 1929, Abbott retourna à New York pour un court séjour. Enthousiasmée par le rythme de cette ville en évolution qui avait été la sienne, elle embarqua son studio pour l'autre coté de l'Atlantique. Tout comme l'ambition d'Atget avait été de garder la mémoire la plus élémentaire d'un certain Paris qu'il adorait et qui disparaissait, Abbott enregistra toutes les images de sa ville sans cesse changeante.

Janet Flanner, Paris, 1927

She began by using a small camera as a sketch pad, noting interesting locations, storefronts, facades, and views, all the while trying to get her portrait business underway. She reserved Wednesdays for exploring the city, concentrating at first on Manhattan island, and later venturing into the outer boroughs, in particular the Bronx and Brooklyn. For her final photographs, she used an 8 x 10-inch view camera, her standard equipment for nearly the rest of her career.

Despite her sound reputation and critical success, the portrait studio upon which she expected to base her livelihood never gained firm financial ground. Abbott found it necessary to seek funds to pursue the New York City documentation project and approached sources such as the Guggenheim Foundation, the Museum of the City of New York, the New York Historical Society, and even private subscription. Titling her proposed project *Changing New York,* Abbott declared that the camera alone could capture the "swift surfaces" of the city and argued that her position as a recently returned American expatriate gave her particular vantage from which to record the changing face of the metropolis.

Zu Beginn benutzte sie eine kleine Kamera gleichsam als Skizzenblock, auf dem sie interessante Details notierte; gleichzeitig bemühte sie sich, als Porträtfotografin ins Geschäft zu kommen. Für ihre Erkundungsgänge in der Stadt hielt sie sich den Mittwoch jeder Woche frei. Zunächst konzentrierte sie sich auf Manhattan, später wagte sie sich sogar in die Bronx und nach Brooklyn. Für die endgültigen Aufnahmen benutzte sie eine 8 x 10-Zoll-Sucherkamera, ihre Standardausrüstung fast bis zum Ende ihres Lebens.

Obwohl sie einen guten Ruf als Fotografin hatte, war ihr Atelier für Porträtaufnahmen finanziell nie erfolgreich genug. Um ihr Dokumentationsprojekt über New York durchführen zu können, mußte Abbott nach Geldgebern suchen. Deshalb wandte sie sich an die Guggenheim Foundation, das Museum of the City of New York, an die New York Historical Society und sogar an Privatleute. Ihr geplantes Projekt nannte sie *Changing New York* und erklärte dazu, daß nur die Kamera in der Lage sei, die »flinken Oberflächen« der Stadt einzufangen und sie, als erst kürzlich zurückgekehrte Amerikanerin, besonders dazu geeignet sei, das sich wandelnde Gesicht der Metropole für die Nachwelt festzuhalten.

Elle commença par utiliser un petit appareil-photo, s'en servant comme d'un bloc-note, elle nota tout ce qui l'intéressait, tout en essayant de faire prospérer son studio de portraits. Les mercredis étaient réservés à l'exploration de la ville, d'abord limitée à Manhattan. Puis elle s'aventura dans les autres quartiers, notamment dans le Bronx et Brooklyn. Pour les photos définitives, elle utilisait un appareil de format 18x24. Ce sera son équipement de base, qu'elle emploiera tout au long de sa carrière.

Malgré sa réputation et le soutien des critiques, le studio de portraits, n'obtint jamais de rentrées d'argent régulières. Abbott dut chercher des fonds pour mener à bien son projet de documentation complète de la ville de New York ; elle en sollicita auprès de sources de financement tels la Guggenheim Foundation, le Museum of the City of New York, la New York Historical Society et même auprès d'éventuels souscripteurs privés. Titrant le projet proposé *Changing New York,* Abbott déclara que seul un appareil-photo peut capter les rapides évolutions de la ville, argumentant sa capacité à fixer les changements par son récent retour aux États-Unis, qui lui donnait un œil particulièrement exacerbé et intéressant pour enregistrer les profils changeants de la métropole.

Jean Cocteau, Paris, 1927

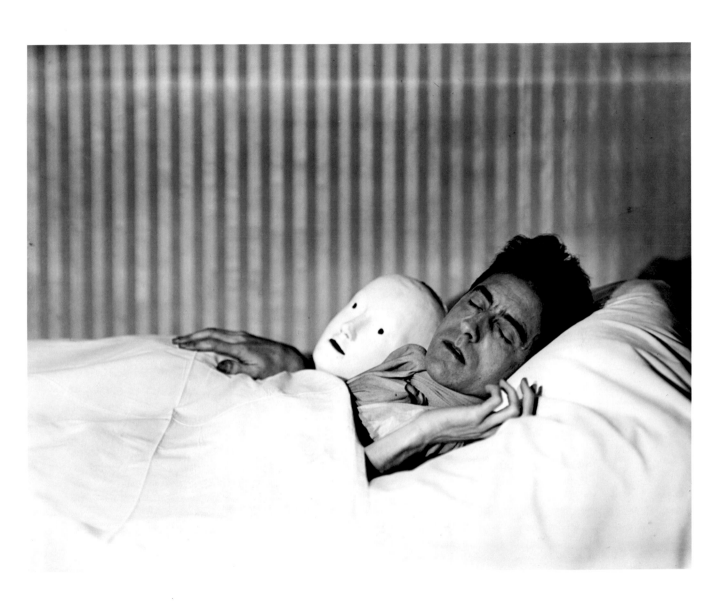

Nevertheless, by 1933, in the midst of the Great Depression, Abbott's appeals for funding had all been rejected. Yet, continuing to work, Abbott gained considerable recognition and respect. Published as early as 1930, her New York City photographs began to be exhibited, first at the Museum of Modern Art, and in 1932 at the opening of the Museum of the City of New York. That museum in 1934 hosted Abbott's first solo exhibition, which led in turn to a life-long friendship with leading art critic Elizabeth McCausland.

Meanwhile, the depression had forced the government to include artists and related workers among the recipients for unemployment relief. While the majority of those involved in the Federal Art Project of the Works Progress Administration were interested in the traditional fine arts media and required photography only as a recording tool, the New York FAP office included a photography section. In 1935 Abbott applied to this organization to carry out *Changing New York*. Her words best explain her motivation and now define her project's success:

Trotzdem blieben bis 1933, dem Höhepunkt der Wirtschaftskrise in den USA, all ihre Finanzierungsgesuche erfolglos. Aber Abbott arbeitete weiter und erlangte nach und nach Anerkennung und Ansehen. Schon 1930 wurden die Fotografien von New York veröffentlicht und anschließend auch auf Ausstellungen gezeigt, zuerst im Museum of Modern Art und 1932 anläßlich der Eröffnung des Museum of the City of New York. Hier fand 1934 auch Abbotts erste Einzelausstellung statt, die zu ihrer lebenslangen Freundschaft mit der Kunstkritikerin Elizabeth McCausland führte.

Inzwischen hatte die Wirtschaftskrise die Regierung dazu gezwungen, auch Künstler und in verwandten Berufen Tätige in ihr Hilfsprogramm für Arbeitslose aufzunehmen. Während die Mehrzahl derjenigen, die an dem Federal Art Project beteiligt waren, sich hauptsächlich für die traditionellen Medien der bildenden Kunst interessierten, gab es im New Yorker FAP-Büro eine Abteilung für Fotografie. Hier stellte Abbott 1935 einen Antrag auf Unterstützung zur Durchführung ihres Projekts *Changing New York*. Ihre eigenen Worte beschreiben am besten ihre Motivation und erklären rückblickend den Erfolg des Projekts:

Mais, en 1933, en plein milieu de la Grande Dépression, les appels de fonds d'Abbott avaient tous échoué. Elle continuait cependant à travailler et gagnait le respect et la reconnaissance des critiques. Publiées dès 1930, ses photographies de New York furent exposées d'abord au Museum of Modern Art, puis, en 1932, au tout nouveau Museum of the City of New York pour son ouverture. Ce musée accueillit sa première exposition personnelle en 1934 ; ce fut aussi le début d'une amitié qui dura toute la vie avec le critique d'art le plus en vue du moment, Elizabeth McCausland.

Pendant cette période de déflation, le gouvernement fut obligé d'inclure les artistes et les travailleurs liés aux arts dans la masse des gens qui percevaient des allocations de chômage. Tandis que la majorité des gens impliqués dans le Federal Art Project ou FAP (Projet artistique fédéral) de ne s'intéressaient qu'aux arts plastiques traditionnels et ne demandaient à la photographie qu'un enregistrement factuel, le bureau du FAP de New York, quant à lui, incluait dans ses départements une section consacrée à la photographie. Abbott s'y présente en 1935 avec *Changing New York*. Ses paroles sont les plus à même de définir sa motivation et d'analyser le succès de son projet :

Nora Joyce, Paris, 1927

"To photograph New York City means to seek to catch in the sensitive and delicate photographic emulsion the spirit of the metropolis, while remaining true to its essential fact, its hurrying tempo, its congested streets, the past jostling the present ... The tempo of the metropolis is not of eternity, nor even time, but of the vanishing instant. Especially then has such a record a peculiarly documentary, as well as artistic, significance. All work that can salvage from oblivion the memorials of the metropolis will have value."

In New York's photography community, still engulfed by Alfred Stieglitz's dominating personality and influence, Abbott's appreciation of temporality and change found little favor. Likewise, Abbott surely felt the strained atmosphere of the art world could only drain the tremendous energy required for her enterprising project. Instead, she found a most suitable champion of her work in I. N. Phelps Stokes, the noted collector of American historical prints and author of the monumental *Iconography of Manhattan Island*. Sitting on the boards of several civic and cultural institutions, he understood the dual artistic and documentary value of

»Die Stadt New York zu fotografieren, bedeutet, den Geist der Metropole auf der höchst empfindlichen fotografischen Emulsion festzuhalten, ohne ihre wesentlichen Merkmale aufzugeben – ihr eiliges Tempo, ihre verstopften Straßen, die enge Nachbarschaft von Vergangenheit und Gegenwart ... Das Zeitmaß der Metropole ist der im Entschwinden begriffene Augenblick. Besonders deshalb hat eine solche Fotografie eine ganz eigentümliche, sowohl dokumentarische als auch künstlerische Bedeutung. Alles, was die Denkmäler der Metropole vor dem Vergessen bewahren kann, wird von Wert sein.«

Die New Yorker Fotografen, die immer noch von Alfred Stieglitz beherrscht wurden, hielten wenig von Abbotts Wertschätzung der Vergänglichkeit und des Wandels. Außerdem erkannte Abbott, daß die gespannte Atmosphäre ihre Energie für das Projekt aufzehren würde. Aber in I. N. Phelps Stokes fand sie einen geeigneten Verfechter ihres Anliegens: Er war ein bekannter Sammler historischer amerikanischer Stiche und der Verfasser des Werks *Iconography of Manhattan Island*. Phelps Stokes saß im Aufsichtsrat verschiedener städtischer und kultureller Institutionen, erkannte den künstlerischen und dokumentarischen Wert von Abbotts Werk und unterstützte ihren Antrag beim FAP.

« Photographier New York, c'est tenter de capturer dans l'émulsion sensible et délicate l'esprit de la ville, tout en restant fidèle aux faits essentiels, son rhythme rapide, ses rues congestionnées, son passé qui coudoie le présent... Le rythme de la métropole n'est pas celui de l'éternité, c'est celui d'un instant qui passe. C'est particulièrement là qu'un tel travail devient une documentation précieuse, relayé par une démarche artistique signifiante. Tout travail qui sauverait la mémoire de la métropole aurait une valeur. »

Dans le milieu new-yorkais de la photographie dominé par l'influence d'Alfred Stieglitz, on accorde à la passion de la temporalité et des variations d'Abbott peu de crédit. Abbott a dû sentir que l'atmosphère stressée du monde artistique ne pourrait que gêner l'aboutissement de ses projets. Elle trouva un admirateur fervent de son travail en I.N. Phelps Stokes, collectionneur acharné de photographies historiques et auteur d'une monumentale *Iconography of Manhattan Island*. Il s'investit dans de nombreuses institutions civiques et culturelles et perçoit l'intérêt artistico-documentaire du travail qu'Abbott cherche à mener à bien ; il soutient sa candidature au FAP de tout son pouvoir.

Eugène Atget, Paris, 1927

the work Abbott sought to complete and strongly supported her FAP application.

Twice during this early period of New York activity Abbott ventured outside the city. In 1933 the noted American architectural historian Henry Russell Hitchcock entrusted her to photograph two of his projects concerning pre-Civil War architecture and the buildings of Boston architect H.H. Richardson, which took her through the cities of the Atlantic seaboard. Two years later, with her friend Elizabeth McCausland, Abbott traveled to the deep south, circling first through Pennsylvania, Ohio, and on to St. Louis. While the resulting work gained additional, if limited, attention, both journeys served more to reinforce her sense of urgency about recording the most dynamic of all American locales, New York.

The fall of 1935 brought not only a commitment from the FAP that was to last for four years, enabling Abbott to hire a small staff and purchase equipment (including a used car), but also her debut as a teacher of photography at the New School for Social Research in New York, the beginning of a happy relationship that was to endure until 1958.

Während dieser ersten Jahre in New York unternahm Abbott zwei Exkursionen. 1933 betraute sie der bekannte amerikanische Architekturhistoriker Henry Russell Hitchcock mit der Aufgabe, Aufnahmen für zwei seiner Bücher zu machen: die Architektur aus der Zeit vor dem amerikanischen Bürgerkrieg und die Bauwerke des Bostoner Architekten H. H. Richardson. Dieser Auftrag führte sie durch die Städte an der Ostküste der Vereinigten Staaten. Zwei Jahre später reiste Abbott mit ihrer Freundin Elizabeth McCausland nach einer Rundfahrt durch Pennsylvania und Ohio bis St. Louis in den tiefen Süden der USA. Diese beiden Reisen verdeutlichten ihr, wie sehr Eile geboten war, den dynamischsten aller amerikanischen Schauplätze, New York, für die Nachwelt festzuhalten.

Der Herbst 1935 war für sie in zweierlei Hinsicht wichtig: Zunächst garantierte ihr das FAP finanzielle Unterstützung für vier Jahre, was Abbott in die Lage versetzte, einen kleinen Mitarbeiterstab einzustellen und Material – u.a. einen Gebrauchtwagen – zu kaufen; außerdem unterrichtete sie erstmals als Dozentin für Fotografie an der New School for Social Research in New York – der Beginn einer glücklichen Verbindung, die bis 1958 bestehenbleiben sollte.

Deux fois pendant cette première période d'activité, Abbott s'aventure hors de New York. En 1933, le célèbre historien de l'architecture Henry Russell Hitchcock lui demande de photographier deux de ses projets, l'un sur l'architecture antérieure à la guerre civile, l'autre sur les immeubles de Boston construits par H.H. Richardson. Ces projets emmènent Berenice Abbott dans des villes du bord de l'Atlantique. Deux ans plus tard, elle repartira, en compagnie de son amie Elizabeth McCausland, pour explorer le Sud profond de Pennsylvanie, en Ohio puis Saint-Louis. Le travail d'Abbott gagna en acuité visuelle et, ces deux voyages renforcèrent son sentiment d'urgence d'enregistrer les images de la scène la plus dynamique de l'Amérique, New York.

L'automne 1935 lui apporte non seulement un engagement de la part du FAP, qui porte sur les quatre années passées et donc lui permet d'une part de s'adjoindre une petite équipe et de racheter du matériel - et même une voiture d'occasion –, et d'autre part de faire ses débuts dans l'enseignement de la photographie à la New School for Social Research à New York. Cet automne-là amène également dans sa vie une nouvelle relation, heureuse - elle durera jusqu'en 1958.

Red River logging project, California, August 1943

In the first two years that she devoted her full effort to *Changing New York* Abbott accomplished much, and in late 1937 produced a solo exhibition at the Museum of the City of New York. The following year publisher E.P. Dutton approached the FAP about a book of New York photographs, and in 1939 brought out *Changing New York,* which included ninety-seven of Abbott's meticulously captioned pictures and historical commentary by Elizabeth McCausland. (It was reprinted in 1973 as *New York in the Thirties.*)

By 1939 the FAP concluded the project and Abbott lost her staff, funding, and finally, her salary. For all practical purposes, she stopped photographing the city, except for new images she made in 1947-48 for *Greenwich Village Today and Yesterday* (1949) with text by Henry Wysham Lanier.

Fortunately, Abbott decided she could rely on her teaching position and the experience of her years in the classroom to write about the methods and philosophy of photography that were so central to her being. Her *Guide to Better Photography* (1941) is an eloquent and powerful document of the best photography of the period, providing great insight

In den ersten beiden Jahren, in denen sie mit ganzer Kraft an *Changing New York* arbeitete, erreichte Abbott viel; und Ende 1937 fand im Museum of the City of New York eine Einzelausstellung statt. Im Jahr darauf wandte sich der Verleger E. P. Dutton an das FAP, und 1939 brachte er *Changing New York* heraus. Es enthielt siebenundneunzig sorgfältig betitelte Fotografien von Abbott und einen historischen Kommentar von Elizabeth McCausland. (1973 erschien eine Neuauflage mit dem Titel *New York in the Thirties.*)

1939 ließ das FAP das Projekt auslaufen, und Abbott stand ohne Mitarbeiter, finanzielle Mittel und ohne Gehalt da. Danach hörte sie praktisch auf, die Stadt zu fotografieren. Nur einmal noch machte sie neue Aufnahmen, und zwar 1947/48 für *Greenwich Village Today and Yesterday,* das 1949 mit einem Text von Henry Wysham Lanier erschien.

Glücklicherweise beschloß Abbott, gestützt auf ihre Dozentenstelle und jahrelange Unterrichtserfahrung, ein Buch über die Methoden und die Philosophie der Fotografie zu schreiben. Ihr *Guide to Better Photography* (1941) ist ein beredtes und eindrucksvolles Dokument der besten Fotokunst jener Zeit, das einen guten Einblick in das große Einfühlungsvermögen er-

Les deux premières années qu'elle a consacrée à son *Changing New York* ont été très fructueuses : en 1937, le Museum of the City of New York lui forge une exposition. L'année suivante, l'éditeur E.P. Dutton approche le FAP pour la publication d'un livre de photos de New York et, en 1939, il publiera *Changing New York,* qui comprendra quatre-vingt dix-sept épreuves d'Abbott méticuleusement légendées et accompagnées d'un commentaire historique de Elizabeth McCausland. (Ce livre a été réimprimé en 1973 sous le titre *New York in the Thirties.*)

En 1939, le FAP met un terme à ses subventions ; Abbott perd son équipe, ses fonds et son salaire. Elle arrête pratiquement de photographier la ville, exception faite d'images nouvelles qu'elle fera en 1947–1948 pour *Greenwich Village Today and Yesterday* (1949), qui seront accompagnées d'un texte de Henry Wysham Lanier.

Fort heureusement, Abbott décide que son travail et son expérience en tant qu'enseignante lui permettent d'écrire sur la philosophie et les techniques de la photographie, si importantes pour elle. Son *Guide to Better Photography* (1941) est un témoignage puissant et éloquent des meilleures photographies de cette période ; d'une perspicacité pénétrante, il per-

Triboro Bridge, East 125th Street approach, June 27, 1937

into an empathetic spirit that Abbott was able to liberate within herself: " ... there is that deeper need for self-expression. In every human being, there are capacities for creative action. ... This need of human beings is almost as deep-seated as their need for air to breathe and food to eat."

At the same time, Abbott stressed the validity of realism as the vehicle for her expression, giving mature and well-considered voice to her enduring commitment to truth:

"As I see straight photography, it means using the medium as itself, not as painting or theater. ... All subject matter is open to interpretation, [and] requires the imaginative and intelligent objectivity of the person behind the camera. The realization comes from selection, aiming, shooting, processing with the best technic possible to project your comment better. ... [Yet] technic for technic's sake is like art for art's sake–a phrase of artistic isolationism, a creative escapism. ... In short, the something done by photography is communication. For what our age needs is a broad, human art, as wide as the world of human knowledge and action; photography cannot explore too far or probe too deeply to meet this need."

möglich, aus dem Abbott schöpfen konnte: »…es gibt ein tieferes Bedürfnis nach Selbstdarstellung. In jedem Menschen liegt die Fähigkeit zu kreativem Tun…Dieses Bedürfnis ist fast so tief im Menschen verwurzelt wie das nach Luft und Nahrung.«

Gleichzeitig bekennt sich Abbott zum Realismus und zu einer unverrückbaren Verpflichtung gegenüber der Wahrheit.

»Ich verstehe unter ehrlicher, ungekünstelter Fotografie, daß man sie als eigenständiges Medium benutzt… Jeder Stoff kann verschieden interpretiert werden und erfordert die phantasievolle und intelligente Objektivität des Menschen hinter der Kamera. Das Bild kommt zustande, nachdem man das Motiv gewählt und die Kamera darauf gerichtet, abgedrückt und es dann mit den besten zur Verfügung stehenden Mitteln entwickelt und kopiert hat, damit man seine Absicht besser vermitteln kann… Aber Technik um der Technik willen ist wie Kunst um der Kunst willen – ein Ausdruck für künstlerische Isolation, kreativen Eskapismus… Fotografie bedeutet Kommunikation. Denn was unsere Zeit braucht, ist eine menschliche Kunst, eine »Breitenkunst«… Um dieses Bedürfnis zu befriedigen, kann die Fotografie nie zu tief schürfen oder ihre Grenzen zu weit abstecken.«

met aussi de comprendre cette incroyable énergie que libérait Abbott : …« il y a ce besoin ancré d'expression de soi. Dans chaque être humain, il y a une capacité d'action créatrice... Ce besoin est aussi profondément enraciné en l'homme que celui d'air pour respirer, ou de la nourriture pour manger. »

Abbott accentuera encore la valeur du réalisme en tant que vecteur de son expression, avec des propos concis sur son engagement à traquer la vérité :

« Ma façon de voir la photographie passe par l'utilisation d'un média en tant que lui-même... Tous les sujets sont ouverts à l'interprétation (et) demandent une objectivité intelligente et imaginative de la personne placée derrière l'appareil. La réalisation vient de la sélection, du but, de la façon de prendre la photo, de travailler pour mieux projeter vers l'extérieur ce que vous avez à dire... (Cela dit) la technique pour la gloire de la technique, c'est comme l'art pour la gloire de l'art - une phrase d'isolation artistique, une échappatoire. En deux mots, ce que fait la photographie, c'est communiquer... Parce que ce dont notre monde a besoin, c'est d'un vaste art humain ; la photographie ne peut fouiller assez profondément pour aller à la rencontre de ce besoin. »

A. J. Corcoran water tanks, New Jersey, 1930

Not only do these comments clearly reflect the tenor of the times - on the brink of the second great war of her generation and rebounding from the slowly expiring effects of the pictorialist movement in photography - they also suggest Abbott's major photographic preoccupation of the next two decades: presenting scientific principles and phenomena photographically.

Eager to find a new arena in which to exploit her talents and energy, Abbott turned to science as the phenomenon of the age most in need of interpretation: "There is an essential unity between photography, science's child, and science, the parent. Yet so far the task of photographing scientific subjects and endowing them with popular appeal and scientific correctness has not been mastered. The function of the artist is needed here, as well as the function of the recorder." Employed by the short-lived *Science Illustrated* in the mid-1940's, she devoted years to seeking interest, and funding, all the while resourcefully devising her own equipment and techniques - garnering several patents - as required by the tasks of depiction she set for herself She also continued to write, speak, teach, and participate fully in the intellectual

Diese Bemerkungen geben nicht nur die allgemeine Einstellung wieder – vor dem Zweiten Weltkrieg zeichnete sich nach der langsam zu Ende gehenden »malerischen« Bewegung eine Gegenbewegung innerhalb der Fotografie ab – , sie deuten auch Abbotts künftiges Hauptanliegen an: die fotografische Darstellung naturwissenschaftlicher Phänomene.

Abbott suchte ein Arbeitsgebiet zu finden, auf dem sie ihrer Begabung und Energie freien Lauf lassen konnte, und wandte sich den Naturwissenschaften zu. »Es besteht eine enge Verbindung zwischen der Fotografie, der Tochter, und ihrer Mutter, der Naturwissenschaft. Aber bisher hat noch niemand die Aufgabe gemeistert, naturwissenschaftliche Objekte zu fotografieren und sie bei aller wissenschaftlichen Korrektheit dennoch einem breiten Publikum interessant erscheinen zu lassen. Hier ist sowohl der Künstler als auch der Dokumentarist gefordert.« Mitte der vierziger Jahre übernahm sie Aufträge für die Zeitschrift *Science Illustrated* – die sich aber nicht lange halten konnte – und bemühte sich jahrelang, für diese Arbeit Interesse zu wecken und Finanzmittel aufzutreiben. Währenddessen entwickelte sie mit großem Einfallsreichtum neue Arbeitsmittel und Techniken, für die sie mehrere

Ces commentaires reflètent, non seulement le cours du temps - peu avant la Seconde Guerre mondiale qui marquera la fin des effets du mouvement pictoral en photographie - ils suggèrent aussi la préoccupation photographique majeure d'Abbott : montrer des principes et des phénomènes scientifiques par le biais de la photographie.

Impatiente de trouver une nouvelle façon d'investir ses talents et son énergie, Abbott se tourne vers la science : « Il y a une unité essentielle entre la photographie, enfantée par la science, et la science elle-même, le parent. Cependant, jusqu'à présent, la photographie de sujets scientifiques et la possibilité de les représenter en les rendant accessibles au grand public tout en leur conservant la justesse scientifique n'a pas été maîtrisée. La fonction artistique est aussi nécessaire ici que la fonction d'enregistrement. » Employée au milieu des années 1940 par le magazine *Science Illustrated,* de courte existence, elle s'acharna des années à susciter l'intérêt et obtenir des fonds. Tout en inventant son propre matériel et en améliorant ses techniques personnelles - elle a déposé plusieurs brevets - comme la tâche qu'elle s'était assignée, celle de montrer, le réclamait. Elle continuait aussi à écrire, à donner des conférences, à

life of the United States. Her *View Camera Made Simple* was published in 1948; *A New Guide to Better Photography* appeared in 1953.

By 1957, the year of Sputnik, the Physical Science Study Committee (composed of MIT scientists and high school science teachers) was hard at work on a new high school physics curriculum that would teach basic principles through experiments and eloquent explanations, both verbal and pictorial. Fortuitously, Abbott's work was well-known by the group's chairman, Dr. E. P. Little, who in 1958 hired her on the spot to provide or create the required illustrative photographs. The skeptics among the group were readily won over by Abbott's professionalism and clear understanding of the subjects' visual requirements.

Engineering her own setups and engaging the talents of her colleagues, Abbott made images that not only picture the phenomena under discussion but also communicate with a photogenic realism peripheral information about the nature of light, the wave force, and magnetism. Well before the seminal textbook *Physics* appeared in 1960, Abbott's images garnered welcome attention and praise. An exhibition

Patente erhielt und nahm intensiv am geistigen Leben der Vereinigten Staaten teil. 1948 wurde ihr Buch *View Camera Made Simple* veröffentlicht, 1953 erschien *A New Guide to Better Photography*.

1957, im Jahr des Sputnik, arbeitete das Physical Science Study Committee, dem Wissenschaftler des Massachusetts Institute of Technology und High-School-Lehrer für naturwissenschaftliche Fächer angehörten, intensiv an einem neuen Lehrplan für den Physikunterricht an High Schools, der die Grundprinzipien der Physik besser veranschaulichen sollte. Der Vorsitzende der Gruppe, Dr. E. P. Little, kannte Abbotts Arbeiten sehr gut und übertrug ihr 1958 die Aufgabe, die zur Illustration nötigen Fotos zu liefern oder neu anzufertigen. Die Skeptiker unter den Mitgliedern des Komitees ließen sich schnell von Abbotts Professionalität und ihrem offensichtlichen Verständnis für die Anforderungen einer anschaulichen Illustrierung überzeugen.

Sie konstruierte selbst die nötigen Geräte und Requisiten, nahm auch die Hilfe von Kollegen in Anspruch und nahm dann Bilder auf, die nicht nur die besprochenen Phänomene darstellten, sondern nebenbei realistisch über die Natur des Lichts, Wellenkraft und Magnetismus infor-

enseigner et à participer pleinement à la vie intellectuelle des États-Unis. Son *View Camera Made Simple* a été publié en 1948 ; *A New Guide to Better Photography* paraît en 1953.

En 1957, l'année du Spoutnik, le Physical Science Study Committee composé de scientifiques du MIT (Massachusetts Institute of Technology) et de professeurs de sciences, travaillait dur sur le programme d'enseignement des sciences en lycée. Cet enseignement devait être fondé sur les principes de base scientifiques. Fortuitement, le travail d'Abbott était connu du président du Comité, le docteur E.P. Little, qui l'engagea sur-le-champ, en 1958, afin de fournir ou de créer les illustrations nécessaires. Les sceptiques du Comité furent gagnés à la cause d'Abbott au vu de son professionnalisme et de sa compréhension visuelle claire des sujets traités.

Fabriquant ses propres décors et s'aidant du talent de ses collègues, Abbott fit des images qui, non seulement montrent les phénomènes traités, mais communiquent également, avec un réalisme artistique, des informations sur la nature de la lumière, de la force des ondes et du magnétisme. Bien avant que soit publié, en 1960, le livre du séminaire, *Physics,* les images d'Abbott ont attiré

was held at the New School and articles appeared in the *New York Times Magazine* and *Art in America,* the latter quoting Abbott: "Surely scientific truth and natural phenomena are as good subjects for art as are man and his emotions, in their infinite variety." The photographs were widely exhibited in schools and science museums, often providing viewers with their first introduction to the world of fine photography. In the 1960's and 1970's Evans G. Valens utilized these photographs in several young peoples' books he put together.

With her work for the PSSC concluded in 1960, Abbott could devote attention again to the Atget archive and to other publishing projects begun earlier. But one important body of work has never been published: In 1954 Abbott twice traveled the length of U. S. 1, the pre-interstate highway linking Maine to Florida, to photograph the vanishing small-town life along the eastern seaboard. The images, with their particularities of subject and great subtlety of viewpoint and light, share with *Changing New York* an ability to function as both documents and art. In their unapologetic realism they provide a moving humanistic and aesthetic counter-

mierten. Schon bevor 1960 das vorbildliche Lehrbuch *Physics* erschien, hatten Abbotts Bilder die Aufmerksamkeit der Öffentlichkeit erregt und viel Lob geerntet. In der New School fand eine Ausstellung statt, und Artikel erschienen im *New York Times Magazine* und in *Art in America.* Im letzteren wird auch Abbott selbst zitiert: »Bestimmt sind wissenschaftliche Wahrheit und Naturphänomene für die Kunst ebenso geeignete Gegenstände wie der Mensch und seine Gefühle in ihrer unendlichen Vielfalt.« Die Fotografien wurden in zahlreichen Schulen und naturkundlichen Museen ausgestellt. In den sechziger und siebziger Jahren nahm Evans G. Valens diese Fotos in viele seiner Bücher für junge Leute auf.

Nachdem 1960 ihre Arbeit für das Physical Science Study Committee beendet war, konnte Abbott sich wieder dem Atget-Archiv und anderen Projekten zuwenden. Aber ein wichtiger Teil ihres Werkes ist nie veröffentlicht worden: 1954 fuhr Abbott zweimal die gesamte U. S. 1 entlang, die Maine mit Florida verband, um das Kleinstadtleben an der Ostküste zu fotografieren. Mit ihrer Fülle an Motiven und dem subtilen Einsatz des Lichtes sind diese Bilder, ebenso wie *Changing New York,* gleichzeitig Dokumentation und Kunst. Ihr Rea-

l'attention. La New School organisa une exposition et des articles parurent dans le *New York Times Magazine,* et dans *Art in America,* ce dernier magazine citant Abbott : « Il est certain que la vérité scientifique et les phénomènes naturels, dans leur infinie variété, sont d'aussi bons sujets que l'homme et ses émotions. » Les photographies furent montrées partout, dans les écoles comme dans les musées scientifiques, offrant souvent un premier contact avec le monde de la photographie artistique. Dans les années 1960 et 1970, Evans G. Valens utilisa bon nombre de ces photographies pour illustrer ses livres pour adolescents.

Son travail avec le Comité s'acheva en 1960. Abbott put revenir aux archives d'Atget et aux autres projets de publication qu'elle avait démarrés précédemment. Mais une partie importante de son travail n'a jamais été publiée : en 1954, Abbott avait voyagé le long de la U. S. 1, route inter-États qui relie la Floride au Maine, et avait photographié la vie éphémère de ces petites villes le long de la côte est. Ces images, avec leurs sujets particuliers et leur intense subtilité de point de vue et de lumière, sont, avec *Changing New York,* des œuvres d'art et des documents précieux. Dans leur réalisme sans anec-

point to the harsher visions of the 1950's.

Once introduced to Maine, Abbott knew she wanted to live there, and in 1956 purchased a run-down roadside inn in Blanchard. Ten years later she moved to her new home for good from her Commerce Street studio in New York. In 1968, in addition to finally settling the disposition of the Atget archive, Abbott and writer Chenoweth Hall produced *A Portrait of Maine* containing Abbott's mostly smaller-format photographs made between 1954 and 1967.

In the 1970's and 1980's, Abbott attained critical standing and financial security, showing her work in several major exhibitions in New York, Washington, and abroad. She also received numerous honorary degrees and awards. A reflective and insightful biography by Hank O'Neal, *Berenice Abbott, American Photographer,* appeared in 1982 with extensive commentary on the photographs by Abbott herself Beginning in 1974, eight portfolios of her photographs were issued, mostly by Parasol Press, and in the mid-1980's an organization called Commerce Graphics was created to manage her archive.

lismus wirkt wie ein anrührend menschlicher und ästhetischer Kontrapunkt gegenüber der verbreiteten harten Sichtweise der fünfziger Jahre.

Als Abbott zum ersten Mal nach Maine kam, erkannte sie sofort, daß sie dort gerne wohnen würde; 1956 kaufte sie in Blanchard ein heruntergekommenes Gasthaus. Zehn Jahre später gab sie ihr Atelier in New York auf und zog für immer in ihr neues Heim. 1968 regelte Abbott schließlich den endgültigen Verbleib des Atget-Archivs und stellte gemeinsam mit der Schriftstellerin Chenoweth Hall den Band *A Portrait of Maine* zusammen. Dieser Band enthält zumeist kleinformatige Fotografien, die zwischen 1954 und 1967 entstanden sind.

In den siebziger und achtziger Jahren erlangte Abbott höchstes Ansehen bei der Kritik und finanzielle Sicherheit, nachdem ihre Arbeiten in New York, Washington und im Ausland gezeigt worden waren. Sie erhielt die Ehrendoktorwürde mehrerer Universitäten und weitere Auszeichnungen. 1982 erschien eine nachdenkliche und einfühlsame Biographie von Hank O'Neal unter dem Titel *Berenice Abbott, American Photographer* mit einem ausführlichen, von Abbott selbst verfaßten Kommentar zu ihren Bildern. Von 1974 an wurden acht Mappen mit ihren Arbeiten veröffent-

dote, elles renferment un humanisme émouvant et apportent un contrepoint esthétique aux visions plus rudes des années 1950.

Dès qu'elle découvrit l'État du Maine, elle sut que c'est là qu'elle voulait vivre. En 1956, elle achète une auberge abandonnée qui se trouve le long d'une route, à Blanchard. Dix ans plus tard, elle y emménage pour de bon, quittant son studio de Commerce Street à New York. En 1968, après avoir réglé tout ce qui concernait les archives d'Atget, Abbott et l'écrivain Chenoweth Hall font *A Portrait of Maine* avec des photos - en majorité des petits formats - qu'elle y a prises entre 1954 et 1967.

Dans les années 1970 et 1980, Abbott atteint enfin la vraie reconnaissance et la sécurité financière, montrant son travail dans plusieurs grandes expositions à New York, à Washington et dans le monde entier. Elle reçoit d'innombrables prix et titres honorifiques. Une biographie sensible et intelligente de Hank O'Neal *Berenice Abbott, American Photographer,* paraît en 1982 ; les photographies sont longuement commentées par Abbott elle-même. A partir de 1974, huit portfolios sortent des presses, la plupart édités par Parasol Press, et, depuis le milieu des années 1980, une organisation, Com-

Cheese shop on West 8th Street, c1949

Abbott remained committed to realism and to the power of the photographic image that speaks for itself The strength she evinced to pursue this vision led to her single-handed rescue of Atget's work and to remarkable technical innovations for the camera. Her legacy resides in six decades of masterful photographs.

Julia Van Haaften

licht, die meisten von Parasol Press; Mitte der achtziger Jahre wurde eine Organisation namens Commerce Graphics zur Betreuung ihres Archivs gegründet.

Abbott fühlte sich weiterhin dem Realismus verpflichtet, sowie der Macht des fotografischen Bildes, das für sich allein spricht. Dank der Kraft, die sie angesichts dieser Vision entwickelte, war sie imstande, ohne fremde Hilfe Atgets Werk zu retten und bemerkenswerte technische Innovationen für die Kamera zu realisieren. Ihr Vermächtnis sind meisterhafte Fotografien aus sechs Jahrzehnten.

Julia Van Haaften

merce Graphics, s'occupe de ses archives.

Abbott est restée fidèle au réalisme et à la puissance de l'image photographique que celle-ci développe d'elle-même. L'énergie qu'elle déploya à la poursuite obstinée de ce qui lui tenait à cœur l'a conduite à sortir le travail d'Atget de l'anonymat et à faire de remarquables innovations techniques en termes de matériel photographique. Elle nous a aussi, et surtout, légué un travail de 60 ans, une œuvre maîtresse.

Julia Van Haaften

Trinidad dancer at the Calypso, Macdougal Street, c1949

Broadway to the Battery, from the roof of Irving Trust Company Building, One Wall Street, May 4, 1938

Designer's window, Bleecker Street, 1947

Union Square, Manhattan, 1936

Trinity Church, New York, 1934

Statue along the tidal basin, Washington D.C., 1954

Exchange Place from Broadway, c1934

Manhattan Bridge, November 11, 1936

Flatiron Building, Broadway and Fifth Avenue, c1934

49

Tempo of the City, Fifth Avenue and 44th Street, 1938

Fifth Avenue Coach Company, 1932

View, Lower Manhattan, 1956

Nightview, New York, 1932

Van de Graff generator, MIT, Cambridge, Massachusetts, 1938

Interference pattern, New York, 1959–61

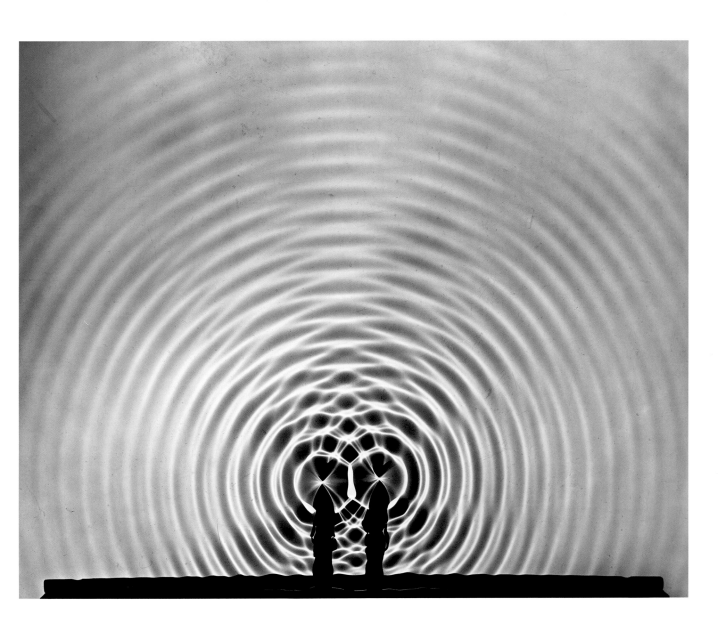

Multiple exposure of bouncing golf ball, New York, 1959–61

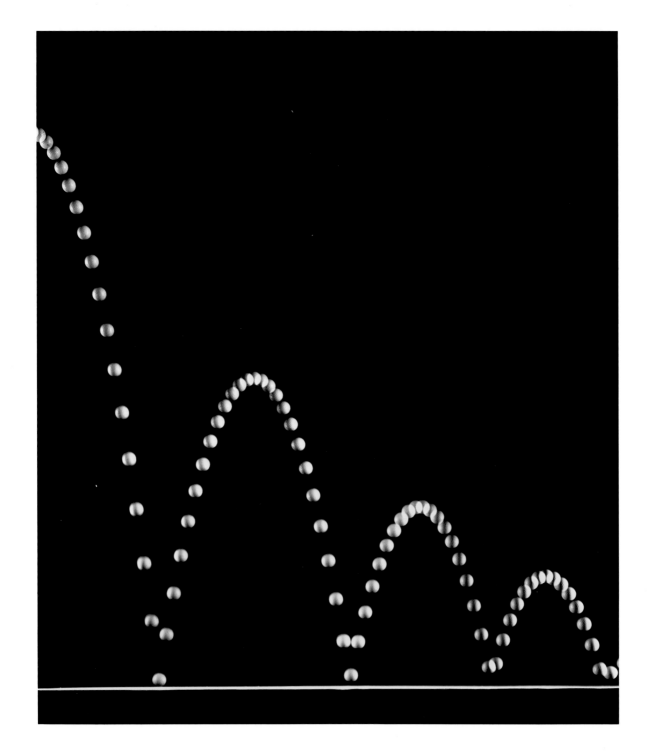

Focusing water waves, MIT, Cambridge, Massachusetts, 1958–61

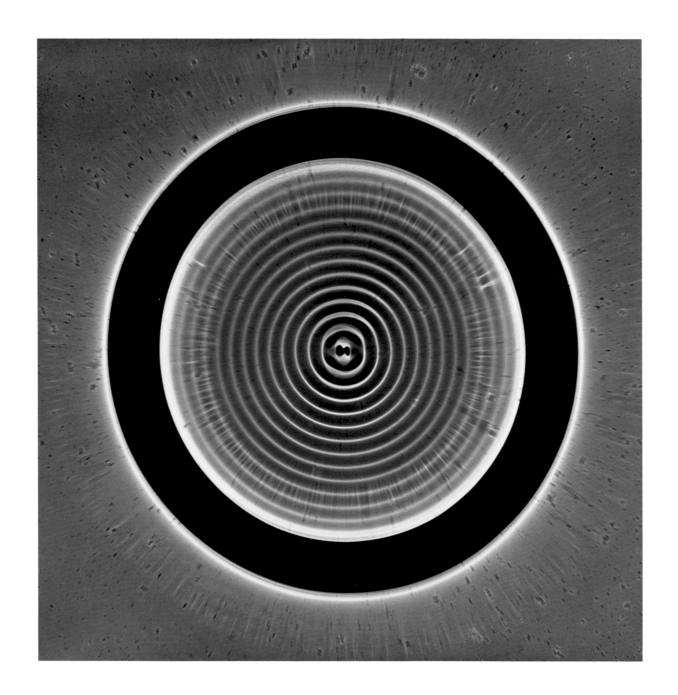

Patterns of the magnetic field, MIT, Cambridge, Massachusetts, 1958–61

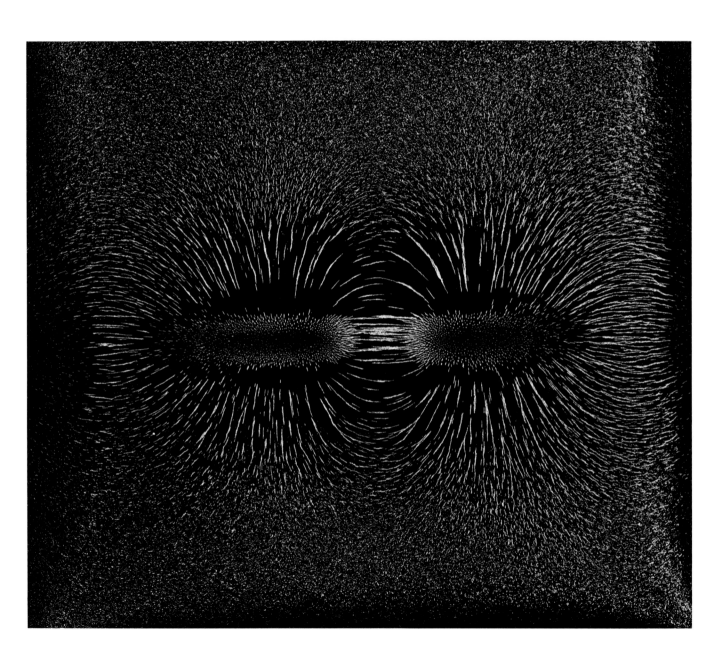

Penicillin mold, MIT, Cambridge, Massachusetts, 1958–61

Light rays through a prism, Cambridge, Massachusetts, 1959–61

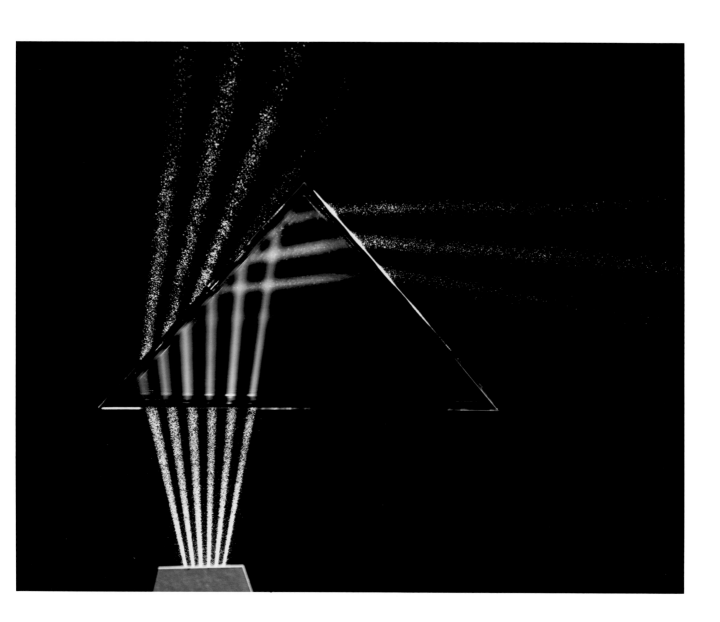

Amusement park, Daytona Beach, Florida, 1954

Prospect Harbor, Maine, c1966

Melbourne Hotel, Melbourne, Florida, 1954

Houses, Newark, New Jersey, 1933

Bonaire Motel, Miami Beach, 1954

Boardwalk, Daytona Beach, Florida, June 23, 1954

Edward Hopper, Greenwich Village, New York, 1947

Milliken's general store on Sunday morning, Bridgewater, Maine, August 22, 1954

BRIEF CHRONOLOGY

1898   BORN July 17, Springfield, Ohio.

1917   LEAVES home to attend Ohio State University with the goal of becoming a journalist.

1918   MOVES to New York City. Interested in sculpture.

1921   SAILS for France.

1923   MOVES to Berlin, returning to Paris after less than a year. Once back in Paris, is hired by Man Ray to work as a darkroom assistant in his portrait business.

1925   BEGINS to make her own photographic portraits. Ends professional commitment to Man Ray and, establishes her own portraiture studio.

1926   VISITS Eugène Atget's studio for the first time. Has her first exhibition at Sacre du Printemps, Paris.

1927   ATGET agrees to allow Abbott to make his portrait. He dies shortly thereafter, and photographs are bequeathed to his Friend André Calmettes.

1928   PURCHASES all of Atget's work from André Calmettes. Exhibits at the first *Salon des indépendants de photographie* with Man Ray, André Kertész, Paul Outerbridge, and Philippe Nadar.

1929   COMES to New York for a brief visit and decides to remain. Establishes a portrait studio, planning to photograph the city in her spare time.

1935   BEGINS teaching photography at the New School for Social Research in New York City. Receives funding from the Federal Art Project, a part of the Works Progress Administration, enabling her to

KURZBIOGRAPHIE

GEBOREN am 17. Juli in Springfield, Ohio.

BEGINN des Studiums an der Ohio State University, Berufsziel: Journalistin.

UMZUG nach New York. Interesse an Bildhauerei.

GEHT nach Frankreich.

UMZUG nach Berlin, nach weniger als einem Jahr Rückkehr nach Paris. Dort erhält sie von Man Ray eine Anstellung als Assistentin im Labor seines Ateliers für Porträtfotografie.

BEGINN eigener Porträtaufnahmen. Aufgabe der Arbeit bei Man Ray, Einrichtung eines eigenen Ateliers für Porträtfotografie.

ERSTER Besuch im Atelier Eugène Atgets. Erste Ausstellung der eigenen Arbeiten bei Sacre du Printemps, Paris.

ATGET gestattet Abbott, Porträtaufnahmen von ihm zu machen. Kurz darauf stirbt er und hinterläßt seinem Freund André Calmettes seine Arbeiten.

ABBOTT kauft André Calmettes das gesamte Werk Atgets ab. Sie stellt im ersten *Salon des indépendants de photographie* aus, zusammen mit Man Ray, André Kertész, Paul Outerbridge und Philippe Nadar.

FÄHRT zu einem Kurzbesuch nach New York und beschließt zu bleiben. Sie eröffnet ein Atelier für Porträtfotografie und plant, in ihrer Freizeit die Stadt zu fotografieren.

BEGINN der Lehrtätigkeit im Fach Fotografie an der New School for Social Research in New York. Vom Federal Art Project der Works Progress Administration zugewiesene Finanzmittel ermögli-

BRÈVE BIOGRAPHIE

NÉE le 17 juillet à Springfield, Ohio.

DÉPART pour l'Université d'État de l'Ohio pour entreprendre des études de journalisme.

PART à New York. S'intéresse à la sculpture.

S'EMBARQUE pour la France.

S'INSTALLE à Berlin pour revenir à Paris après moins d'un an. De retour à Paris, elle travaille pour Man Ray en tant qu'assistante de chambre noire dans son studio de portraits.

COMMENCE à faire elle-même des portraits. Arrête la collaboration professionnelle avec Man Ray et monte son propre studio photo.

FAIT la connaissance d'Eugène Atget. Sa première exposition personnelle se tient au Sacre du Printemps à Paris.

ATGET accepte qu'Abbott fasse des portraits de lui. Il meurt peu après, et les photographies sont léguées à son ami André Calmettes.

ACHÈTE toute l'œuvre d'Atget à André Calmettes. Expose au premier *Salon des indépendants de photographie* avec Man Ray, André Kertész, Paul Outerbridge et Philippe Nadar.

BRÈVE visite à New York. Décide d'y revenir et monte un studio de portrait qui lui laissait la possibilité de photographier la ville pendant ses loisirs.

DÉBUTE l'enseignement de la photographie à la New York School for Social Research à New York City. Reçoit des subventions du Federal Art Project, un département de la WorksProgress

Milliken's general store on Sunday morning, Bridgewater, Maine, August 22, 1954

photograph on a full time basis, and begin her project *Changing New York*.

1937 ATGET'S photographs exhibited at the Museum of Modern Art.
1938 LEARNS of Lewis Hine and attempts to help him gain recognition for his photographs.
1939 RESIGNS from the Federal Art Project. Decides that her next project will show the links between science and art and begins fundraising.
1940 BEGINS experimentation with wave form photographs.
1942 INVENTS *Projection Supersight System*.
1944 TAKES position as photo editor at *Science Illustrated*.
1945 RESIGNS from her position at *Science Illustrated* under its new management.
1947 FOUNDS House of Photography to market and patent her inventions.
1951 "IT has to walk alone ..." statement made at the Aspen Institute for Humanistic Studies in Colorado.
1954 PHOTOGRAPHING expedition with Elizabeth McCausland along Route 1 between Maine and Florida.
1956 PURCHASES land in Blanchard, Maine.
1958 RETIRES From her position at the New School for Social Research. Joins Physical Science Study Committee (P.S.S.C.) of Educational Services, Inc. in Cambridge, Massachusetts. Photographs scientific

chen es ihr, sich ganz auf die Fotografie zu konzentrieren und mit ihrem Projekt *Changing New York* zu beginnen.

AUSSTELLUNG der Fotografien Atgets im Museum of Modern Art.
HÖRT von Lewis Hine und versucht, ihm Anerkennung für seine Fotografien zu verschaffen.
AUFGABE der Arbeit beim Federal Art Project. Entschluß, als nächstes Projekt die Verbindung zwischen Naturwissenschaft und Kunst sichtbar zu machen; Bemühung um Fördermittel.
EXPERIMENTIERT mit dem Fotografieren von Wellen.
ERFINDUNG des *Projection Supersight System*.
BILDREDAKTEURIN bei der Zeitschrift *Science Illustrated*.
ENDE der Beschäftigung bei *Science Illustrated*, als die Leitung der Zeitschrift wechselt.
GRÜNDUNG des House of Photography zum Vertrieb und zur Patentierung ihrer Erfindungen.
»IT has to walk alone . . .« (etwa: »Die Fotografie muß auf eigenen Füßen stehen«): am Aspen Institute for Humanistic Studies, Colorado, von Abbott vertretene These.
FOTOEXPEDITION zusammen mit Elizabeth McCausland entlang der Route 1 zwischen Maine und Florida.
GRUNDERWERB in Blanchard (Maine).
AUFGABE der Stelle an der New School for Social Research. Mitglied des Physical Science Study Committee (P.S.S.C.) der Educational Services, Inc., in Cambridge (Massachusetts). Innovative Fotografien

Administration qui lui permet de photographier la ville à plein temps et démarre son projet *Changing New York*.

LES PHOTOGRAPHIES d'Atget sont exposées au Museum of Modern Art.
ENTEND parler de Lewis Hine et tente de faire reconnaître son travail photographique.
LES SUBVENTIONS du Federal Art Project sont coupées. Décide que son prochain projet montrera les liens entre science et art et commence à chercher des subventions.
COMMENCE à expérimenter les longueurs d'ondes en photographie.
INVENTE le *Projection Supersight System*.
DEVIENT directrice photo à *Science Illustrated*.
QUITTE *Science Illustrated* qui a changé de comité de direction.
FONDE la House of Photography pour breveter et vendre ses inventions.
« IL faut qu'il marche tout seul... » déclaration faite à l'Aspen Institute for Humanistic Studies dans le Colorado.
EXPÉDITION photographique avec Elizabeth McCausland le long de la Route 1 entre les États du Maine et de la Floride.
ACHÈTE un terrain à Blanchard, Maine
CESSE l'enseignement à la New School for Social Research. Rejoins le Physical Science Study Committee (P.S.S.C.) of Educational Services inc., à Cambridge, Massachusetts. Photographie les principes

principles in innovative ways, many the first photographs of certain phenomena.

1959 VOTED one of the Top Ten Women Photographers in the United States by the Professional Photographers of America.

1960 THE SMITHSONIAN Institution takes on the circulation management of the PSSC photographs; most were Abbott's.

1962 MOVES to her property in Maine.

1968 ATGET collection is sold to the Museum of Modern Art.

1971 AWARDED honorary doctorate from the University of Maine.

1973 AWARDED honorary doctorate From Smith College.

1981 RECEIVED the Association of International Photo Art Dealers award for Outstanding Contribution to the Field of Photography.

1982 A MOVIE about Abbott's work, directed by Erwin Leiser, is released.

1986 AWARDED honorary degree from Ohio State University.

1987 AWARDED The First International Erice Prize for Photography.

1988 INDUCTED into Order of Arts and Letters by the French Government.

1991 DIES 9 December of heart faieure.

---

naturwissenschaftlicher Prinzipien; viele Phänomene werden hiermit erstmals fotografiert.

WAHL der Professional Photographers of America fällt auf Abbott als eine der Top Ten Women Photographers der USA.

DIE SMITHSONIAN Institution übernimmt die Verwaltung und Betreuung der PSSC-Fotos; die Mehrzahl davon stammt von Abbott.

UMZUG in ihr Haus in Maine.

VERKAUF des Atget-Archivs an das Museum of Modern Art.

VERLEIHUNG der Ehrendoktorwürde durch die University of Maine.

VERLEIHUNG der Ehrendoktorwürde durch das Smith College.

AUSZEICHNUNG der Association of International Photo Art Dealers für »Outstanding Contribution to the Field of Photography« (»hervorragende Leistungen auf dem Gebiet der Fotografie«).

FILM über Abbotts Werk (Regie: Erwin Leiser).

VERLEIHUNG eines akademischen Ehrengrades durch die Ohio State University.

VERLEIHUNG des First International Erice Prize for Photography.

AUSZEICHNUNG der französischen Regierung mit dem Orden für Kunst und Wissenschaft.

STIRB am 9. Dezember an Herzversagen.

---

scientifiques en innovant ; ses photographies sont souvent les premières à fixer certains phénomènes.

ÉLUE une des dix meilleures photographes aux États-Unis par les Professional Photographers of America.

LE SMITHSONIAN Institution prend en charge la circulation des photos du PSSC; la plupart d'entre elles sont d'Abbott.

S'INSTALLE dans sa maison du Maine.

L'ŒUVRE photographique d'Atget est vendue au Museum of Modern Art

NOMMÉE docteur honoris causa de l'Université du Maine.

NOMMÉE docteur honoris causa du Smith College.

REÇOIT le prix de l'Association of International Photo Art Dealers pour sa collaboration marquante dans le champ de la Photographie.

UN film sur l'œuvre d'Abbott, réalisé par Erwin Leiser, sort sur les écrans.

OBTIENT un grade honoraire de Université d'État de l'Ohio.

OBTIENT le First International Erice Prize for Photography.

OBTIENT la distinction de Chevalier des Arts et Lettres du gouvernement français.

MEURT le 9 décembre d'une défaillance cardiaque.

1926 Au Sacre du Printemps, Paris.

1930 Contemporary Art Club, Harvard University.

1934 New School for Social Research; Museum of the City of New York; Yale University.

1935 Smith College; Museum of Fine Arts, Springfield, Massachusetts.

1937 Museum of the City of New York; Yale University.

1938 Hudson D. Walker Gallery, New York City.

1939 Federal Art Gallery; Museum of Modern Art, New York City.

1941 Massachusetts Institute of Technology.

1947 Galérie l'Époque, Paris.

1950 Akron Art Institute, Akron, Ohio.

1951 The Art Institute of Chicago.

1953 Caravan Gallery, New York City; San Francisco Museum of Modern Art.

1955 Currier Art Gallery, Manchester, New Hampshire.

1956 Toronto Art Museum.

1959 Massachusetts Institute of Technology, Faculty Club; New School for Social Research.

1960 Smithsonian Institution, exhibits Physical Sciences Study Committee photographs for touring exhibition.

1970 Museum of Modern Art, New York City.

1971 University of Maine, Augusta.

1973 Witkin Gallery, New York City.

1975 Focus Gallery, San Francisco.

1976 Marlborough Gallery, New York City.

1977 Treat Gallery, Bates College, Lewiston, Maine.

1979 Provincetown Fine Arts Workshop.

1980 *Changing New York,* Galerie zur Stockeregg, Zurich.

1981 *The 20's and 30's,* International Center of Photography, New York.

1982 Smithsonian Institution.

1985 *Vision of the Twentieth Century,* Massachusetts Institute of Technology Museum.

1986 Ikona Gallery, Venice, Italy.

1987 *The Beauty of Physics,* Academy of Sciences, New York.

1988 *Foto Fest,* Heritage Plaza, Houston; Silver Image Gallery, Seattle, Washington; Heckscher Museum, Huntington, New York.

1989 I.C.P. New York. Galerie zur Stockeregg, *Zürich Ferderal art project changing New York.* New York Public Library, New York.

1993 *B.A. Ferderal Art Project 1935–39 New York,* Metropolitan Museum of New York; Anita Neugebauer, Basel.

1994 FNAC Montparnasse, Paris *New York 1930.*

1995 Photographers' Gallery, London *Portraits 1925–1930.*

1996 I.C.P. New York *Portraits, New York Views, and science Photographs from the Permanent Collection.*

Albert and Vera List Visual Arts Center, MIT, Cambridge, Massachusetts

Allen Memorial Act Museum

Art Institute of Chicago

Bibliothèque Nationale, Paris

Chase Manhattan Bank, New York

Detroit Institute of Arts

Fogg Art Museum, Harvard University, Cambridge, Massachusetts

High Museum of Art, Atlanta

Indiana University Art Museum, Bloomington

International Museum of Photography/George Eastman House, Rochester, New York

Menil Foundation, Houston, Texas

Metropolitan Museum of Art, New York

Minneapolis Institute of Arts, Minnesota

Museum of the City of New York

Museum of Fine Arts, Boston

Museum of Fine Arts, Houston

Museum of Modern Art, New York

New York Public Library

San Francisco Museum of Modern Art

Wellesley College Museum, Wellesley, Massachusetts

Yale University Art Gallery, New Haven, Connecticut

House Belfast, Maine along Route 1, 1954

SELECTED BIBLIOGRAPHY
AUSGEWÄHLTE BIBLIOGRAPHIE
SÉLECTION BIBLIOGRAPHIQUE

BOOKS BY
BERENICE ABBOTT
BÜCHER VON
BERENICE ABBOTT
LIVRES DE
BERENICE ABBOTT

The Attractive Universe, text by E. G.
   Valens, Cleveland: World Publishing
   Company, 1969.
Photographs, New York: Horizon Press,
   1970.
The Red River Photographs, text by Hank
   O'Neal, Provincetown, 1979.
Changing New York, text by Elizabeth
   McCausland, New York: E. P. Dutton
   and Company, 1939. Reprinted as:
   New York in the Thirties, New York:
   Dover Publications, Inc., 1973.
Greenwich Village Today and Yesterday, text
   by Henry Wysham Lanier, New York:
   Harper and Brothers, 1949.
A Guide to Better Photography, New York:
   Crown Publishers, 1941.
Magnet, text by E. G. Valens, Cleveland:
   World Publishing Company, 1964.
Motion, text by E. G. Valens, Cleveland:
   World Publishing Company, 1965.
A New Guide to Better Photography, New
   York: Crown Publishers, 1953.
A Portrait of Maine, text by Chenoweth
   Hall, New York: The Macmillan
   Company, 1968.
The View Camera Made Simple, Chicago:
   Ziff-Davis, 1948.
The World of Atget, New York: Horizon
   Press, 1964.

SELECTED ARTICLES BY
BERENICE ABBOTT
AUSGEWÄHLTE ARTIKEL VON
BERENICE ABBOTT
ARTICLES SELECTIONNÉS DE
BERENICE ABBOTT

Abbott, Berenice. "Documenting the
   City," *The Complete Photographer,* 1942,
   No. 22. Reprinted in the *Encyclopedia
   of Photography,* 1963, vol. 7.
—. "Eugene Atget," *Creative Art,*
   September, 1929.
—. "Eugene Atget," *The Complete
   Photographer,* 1941, No. 6. Reprinted in
   the *Encyclopedia of Photography,* 1963,
   Vol. 2.
—. "My Favorite Picture," *Popular
   Photography,* February, 1940.
—. "My Ideas on Camera Design,"
   Popular Photography, May, 1939.
—. "The Image of Science," *Art in
   America,* 1959, 47:4.
—. "It Has to Walk Alone," *Infinity,*
   1951, Vol. 7, pp. 6-7,11.
—. "Lisette Model," *Camera,* 1975, pp. 4,
   21.
—. *Lisette Model,* photographs by Lisette
   Model, introduction by Berenice
   Abbott, Millerton: Aperture, 1979.
—. "Nadar: Master Portraitist," *The
   Complete Photographer,* 1943, No. 51.
—. "Photographer as Artist," *Art Front,*
   1936, Vol. 16.
—. "Photography 1839-1937," *Art Front,*
   1937, Vol. 17.
—. "Photography at the Crossroads,"
   Universal Photo Almanac, 1951, pp. 42-
   47.
—. "View Cameras," *The Complete
   Photographer,* 1943, No. 53.

—. "What the Camera and I See,"
   ARTnews, 1951, Vol. 50, p. 5.
—. "Photography and Science," written
   in New York, 1939.

SELECTED ARTICLES ABOUT
BERENICE ABBOTT
AUSGEWÄHLTE ARTIKEL ÜBER
BERENICE ABBOTT
ARTICLES SELECTIONNÉS SUR
BERENICE ABBOTT

"Abbott's Non-Abstract Abstracts,"
   Infinity, 1962, Vol. 11, p. l.
Bell, Madeline. "Changing New York,"
   Springfield Sunday Union and Republican,
   April 23, 1939.
"Berenice Abbott Photographs the Face
   of a Changing City," *Life,* January 13,
   1938.
Berman, Avis. "The Pulse of Reality -
   Berenice Abbott." *Architectural Digest,*
   April, 1985, Vol. 42, p. 74.
— "The Unflinching Eye of Berenice
   Abbott," *Art News,* January 1981, Vol.
   80, pp. 86-93.
Deschin, Jacob. "Viewpoint: Award to
   Berenice Abbott," *Popular Photography,*
   December 1981, Vol. 88, p. 46.
Katz, Leslie George. "Berenice Abbott As
   a Pioneer," *Berenice Abbott,* lkona
   Gallery Exhibition Catalogue, Venice,
   Italy, June, 1987.
Kramer, Hilton. "Vanished City Life by
   Berenice Abbott on View," *New York
   Times,* November 27, 1981, sec. 3, p.1.
Larson, K. "Abbott and Atget," *New
   Yorker,* December 1981, Vol.14, pp.
   150-151.
Lifson, Ben. "The Woman who Rescued
   Atget's Work," *Saturday Review,*

October 1981, pp. 30-31.

McCausland, Elizabeth. "The Photography of Berenice Abbott," *Trend,* March-April 1935, Vol. 3, p. l.

— "Berenice Abbott-Realist," *Photo Arts,* 1948, Vol. 2, p. l.

Newman, Julia. "Berenice Abbott - Pioneer, Past and Present," *U.S. Camera,* February, 1960.

"Picture This Career," *Mademoiselle,* August, 1934.

Reilly, Rosa. "Berenice Abbott Records Changing New York," *Popular Photography,* Vol. 3, p. 3, September, 1938.

Starenko, M. "I to Eye-Self-Portrait: The Photographer's Persona 1840-1985" [M.O.M.A. exhibition review] *Afterimage,* January 1986, Vol. 13, p. 17.

Steiner, Ralph. "Berenice Abbott," *PM,* April 19, 1942.

Sundell, Michael G. "Berenice Abbott's Work in the Thirties," *Prospects: An Annual of American Cultural Studies* 5,1980, pp. 269-292.

Zwingle, E. "A Life of Her Own," *American Photographer,* April 1986, Vol. 16, pp. 54-67.

APERTURE MASTERS OF PHOTOGRAPHY